To Todd

From Your Sunday School Teacher

DEVOTIONS
for Preteens
No. 5

LISTENING TO GOD
WITH PAUL

Original Title:
LISTENING TO GOD

Mary Lillian Miles

John Miller
1979

MOODY PRESS

CHICAGO

1972 Edition
ISBN: 0-8024-3225-5

Printed in the United States of America

Preface

This book of devotions is written for the purpose of encouraging teen-agers and even preteens to have their own daily quiet time with God. Having found it difficult to interest my children in the reading of the Bible for themselves, I felt that what they needed was a planned course of readings, with a brief, pointed application.

The readings are also helpful for family worship.

In a previous book, *My Quiet Time with God*, I covered Acts. The present volume uses short, simple passages from the Pauline epistles. Using a title, explanation, and closing thrust (thought for the day or poem), I have endeavored to interpret the Bible passage in terms of everyday life on a young person's level.

Foreword

The book is dedicated to young people everywhere with the earnest hope that through the
daily reading of God's precious Word they may
"grow in grace, and in the knowledge of our
Lord and Saviour Jesus Christ."

Having read the life of the great missionary,
Paul, in the Book of Acts, I am sure you would
like to read parts of some of the letters he wrote
to the people he brought to the Lord Jesus. We
call these letters "epistles."

Try to get Frank Laubach's *The Inspired Letters,* or J. B. Phillips' *Letters to Young Churches,*
or his translation of the New Testament. The
language of these books is easier to understand
than the older language used in the Authorized
Version of the Bible, which you may be using
now. Dr. Laubach and Dr. Phillips have trans-
lated the Bible into the language which we use
today.

Each day before you read the Bible portion
you may like to use this little prayer:

> Dear Lord, open my eyes that I may
> see wonderful things in Your Word, and
> and open my heart to receive the truth.

4

Romans

The Get-Acquainted Letter

It was while Paul was staying in the city of Corinth that he wrote this letter to the Christians in Rome. You can easily find Rome on any map of Europe. It is the capital of Italy, the country that looks like a boot. Paul hadn't been to Rome yet when he wrote this letter, but how he longed to see the Christians there (Acts 19:21b)! He was what we call a pioneer missionary. His special work was to take the Gospel message to places where no other missionary had ever been. So far as we know, no missionary had ever been to Rome. The Church had been started by Christians who came from other places to live there. It was to them that Paul wrote this "get-acquainted" letter, promising them that he would pay them a visit as soon as possible. It is a wonderful letter. We'll pick out a few of the most interesting parts.

READ ROMANS 1:7-10, 14-16.

Paul's Debt and Mine

"Dear John"—that's how you begin a letter, and we call it the "salutation." Verse 7 is the salutation of this long letter, and what a beautiful one it is! If you are saved, you too are "beloved of God" and to you He gives grace and peace. But this wonderful peace is not given to you so that you may just hug it to yourself. Like Paul, you are in debt. That means you owe the Gospel message to those who don't know the Lord. Paul knew this, and he wrote: "I am *eager* [ready] to pay my debt [v. 15], and I am not ashamed [v. 16] to tell little people and big people alike, because I know the Gospel is able to change lives." Are you paying your debt to your neighbor, your friends? Maybe someday you'll be a missionary like Paul and pay your debt to those in other lands.

SONG FOR TODAY:

> I love to tell the story, 'tis pleasant to repeat,
> What seems, each time I tell it, more wonderfully sweet.

6

I love to tell the story, for some have never
    heard
The message of salvation from God's own
    holy Word.

A Gift Worth Taking

When I was a little girl I remember a children's meeting that I attended where the speaker asked, "Is there a boy or girl here who has never done anything wrong?" One girl raised her hand and insisted that she had never done wrong in all her life. Most people know that in God's sight they are certainly not perfect, but a great many think that if they do the best they can, they will earn their way into Heaven. But forgiveness is a gift; you can't do anything to earn it. You get a gift by receiving it, don't you? That's what faith is—it is believing that Jesus died for you and receiving Him as your Saviour. When we do that, we are *justified*. What does that mean? It means, "Just as if I had never sinned." Think of it! That's a gift worth taking. And since we didn't earn it, there's nothing to brag about, is there?

Today's Thought:

A gift is free to the one who receives it, but *someone* has to pay for it. The gift of our salvation cost the Lord Jesus His death on the cross.

Read Romans 4:3, 20-25.

Something You Can't Earn

It made the Jews angry when Paul preached that no one can earn salvation, because they thought they were better than other people. Paul showed them that even Abraham, the father of their nation, was not saved by his good works but by his faith. God had told him that he was going to have children and grandchildren and great-grandchildren until there were too many even to count. Well, how many children did he have when God made this promise? Not a single one. Worse still, he and his wife were too old to have children. Yet he did not doubt for a minute that God was able to do what He had promised. And God said, "Abraham, because you trust me fully, I will forgive all your sins and count you as a good man." Verses 23 and 24 tell us that if we believe that Jesus died for our sins and rose again, God will forgive us too, and count us good.

A Bible Verse for Today:

Blessed are they that have not seen [Jesus], and yet have believed.—John 20:29

9

Something No One Deserves

A mother and father will gladly die for their children. A friend will sometimes die for a friend. But did you ever hear of anyone dying for an enemy? Yes, I heard of Someone who did just that—the Lord Jesus. How wonderful is God's love! He gave His only Son to die for us though we did not love Him at all! When we take Him as our Saviour He gives us peace, deep, sweet peace; and He pours His love into our hearts. With His peace and love filling us, we can be happy even when trials and sorrows (tribulations) come. "Hope" in verse 4 isn't a "maybe"; here it means "we know for sure." We not only hope; we *know* that nothing can separate us from God's love, and that some day we shall share in the glories of Heaven.

A BIBLE VERSE TO MEMORIZE:

> But God proves His love for us by the fact that Christ died for us while we were still sinners.—Romans 5:8, Williams' Translation

READ ROMANS 6:11-14.

Are You Your Own Boss?

If you're a Christian and you are trying to run your own life, I am quite sure you are making a sad mess of it. Because, you see, you aren't strong enough to live a life that is pleasing to God, no matter how hard you try. Don't be shocked at my question, Is Satan the boss? Do you listen when he whispers temptations into your mind? If you do, you're letting sin rule you, and you are obeying Satan. God doesn't expect unsaved people to obey Him, but if we have taken Jesus as our Saviour, we should also determine to obey Him. We should give Him our hands and feet, our eyes and ears and mouths. The secret of victory over every temptation is to give ourselves *wholly* to Jesus over and over again each day, and to turn a deaf ear to the whisperings of Satan.

A PRAYER POEM:

> I'll do what You tell me to do, dear Lord.
> I'll say what You want me to say.
> No longer for self and sin I'll live—
> Your voice I will always obey.

—M. L. M.

READ ROMANS 7:18-25a.

Paul's Tongue Twister

We find the tongue twister in verse 19: What I do want to do, I don't do; and what I do not want to do, I do. Just as soon as we become Christians and begin to live a new life, the fight is on. We had thought it would be easy to be good once we were saved, but before very long we have found out that there's nothing good in us. The new Mary longs to please Jesus, but the old Mary is at war with the new Mary, and often wins. Like Paul, we are at our wits' end and we say sadly, "Oh, dear, how can I ever win the battle with my old, sinful self!" And the answer is right here in verse 25. The Lord Jesus can break the chains of sin which bind me. So I must stop struggling and learn to trust Him moment by moment.

A BIBLE VERSE FOR TODAY:

> Thanks be to God which giveth us the victory through our Lord Jesus Christ.— I Corinthians 15:57

My Father

Those who do not know God as a loving Father are often afraid of Him. The heathen sometimes call Him "the Great Spirit," and they live in fear of Him all the time because they think that He will surely punish them for their sins. How thankful we should be that probably ever since we can remember we have heard in songs and stories that God loves us and sent His Son to die so that we may have forgiveness and become the children of God! When you learned to talk, what word did you say first? Perhaps it was "Da-da." When we accept Jesus as our Saviour and are born into God's family, our first word is "Father." How wonderful to know the great Creator of the world as our Father! We may have troubles here, but they're nothing compared to the joys that are waiting for us in our Father's Home.

TODAY'S THOUGHT:

> If I'm a child of the heavenly Father, I
> want to live so that others can tell I belong
> to His family.

13

READ ROMANS 8:28, 31-34.

Troubles Turn into Blessings

Is something troubling you right now? If it's some wrong thing you have done, you know how to get forgiveness and peace (I John 1:9). But if it's something you couldn't help, cheer up! God tells us in His Word that this trouble is going to turn into a blessing for you *if you love Him*. No, I didn't say that the trouble is good. No trouble is good; but God makes it work in with other things so that it turns out for our good. If God is on our side, nothing at all, no one in all the world can really do us harm. God gave His only Son to die for us, so He won't go back on His Word and charge us with sin. Jesus who died for us is now praying for us in Heaven; He won't blame us for the sins which He has already forgiven. How wonderful to be in the sheltering love of our heavenly Father!

A BIBLE VERSE TO MEMORIZE:

We *know* that all things work together for good to them that love God.—Romans 8:28

READ ROMANS 8:35-39.

His Forever

A mother robin built a nest high up in the branches of an old oak tree. The tree grew on the side of a steep cliff above the ocean. One day when the baby birds were tiny, a great storm arose. The wind whipped the waves so that they rose in dark, high ridges tipped with foam, and dashed madly against the cliff. The branches of the old oak creaked and groaned as the wind tore angrily at them. But deep within that little nest of straw the baby birds nestled under their mother's sheltering wings. They heard the noise of the storm, but were not the least bit afraid, for they knew their mother would never leave them while the storm raged. You and I are sheltered in the love of our dear Saviour. Not anyone, nor anything, past, present, or yet to come, can cut off His love for us—not even the Devil himself.

> Under His wings, under His wings,
> Who from His love can sever?
> Under His wings my soul shall abide,
> Safely abide forever.
> —By permission of Hope Publishing Company

READ ROMANS 10:9-13.

How to Be Saved

Some people go to Sunday school and church for years, yet they never find just how to be saved. They only *hope* they are saved. Could this be you? Well, here it is, so simple that a small child can understand. It means 1) believing with all your heart that Jesus is *Lord,* God's holy Son, and that He rose from the dead (v. 9b). And of course, if He rose from the dead, His death was no ordinary death. He died for our sins, as He said He would. All right, you say you already believe this; that you not only know it in your head, but believe it in your heart. Wait a minute, that's not quite enough; 2) you must ask Him to be *your* Saviour. That's what verse 13 says, doesn't it? And that's one way of "confessing" that Jesus is Lord, telling Him you want Him to be *your* Lord. Then tell someone else too. You've believed in Him and called on Him? Then you're saved, because God can't lie. His Word is true.

Whosoever shall call upon the name of
the Lord shall be saved.—Romans 10:13

16

Read Romans 10:14, 15.

Beautiful Feet

We never think of feet as beautiful, do we? But God does (v. 15). You see, He sent His only Son from Heaven to earth to die for our sins. The Lord Jesus told His followers plainly that they could be saved by believing in Him and calling on Him, as we read yesterday. After Jesus rose from the dead, He told His followers that He was going back to His Father's Home. He said it would be up to them to tell others about Him. If they had kept the Good News to themselves, you and I would be heathen people, worshiping idols. But there are still heathen people who have never heard the Good News. How shall they ever hear unless someone goes to tell them? We can't all go to faraway lands, but if God speaks to our heart and says, "I want to send *you*," we should be willing to say, "Here I am, send me."

> Here am I, O Lord, send me!
> Many have not heard of Thee.
> Willing now to go or stay,
> I will serve Thee every day.
>
> —M. L. M.

READ ROMANS 12:1-5.

New Minds

Imagine what it would be like if each part of our body did just as it pleased! One leg might want to walk one way, and the other leg another way. In order to be sensible, useful people, every part of our bodies must obey our head. Now every Christian is a part of a great body of God's people, and the Lord Jesus is our Head. So you see why it is so important for every single one of us to say, "Lord, I give myself entirely to You. From now on I won't do just as I please. I'll do what You want me to do." When we think of all He has done for us, it is the least we can do, isn't it? How can we know what He wants us to do? We must ask Him for a new mind, a mind that doesn't want to please ourselves, a mind like that of the Lord Jesus who said to His Father, "I delight to do thy will, O my God" (Ps. 40:8).

TODAY'S THOUGHT:

> I'm only a small part of a great body of God's people, so there's no reason why I should have big ideas about myself.

18

READ ROMANS 12:6-13.

Give with a Big Heart

Some parts of our bodies have very important work to do, and other parts have smaller jobs; but we need all of them, right down to our little finger. The thing that counts is not how big a job I do, but how well I do what is expected of me. Tucked in among the list of "gifts" which God has given different ones, so that they may serve Him, is the gift of giving. We can all serve God by being generous, even though we may never be able to teach a class or preach a sermon. And Paul says, if you're going to give for Jesus' sake, "give with a big heart" (Laubach). Then follow thirteen short rules, beginning with a very important one: "Let your love be *real*" (v. 9, Laubach). Let us never pretend to love the Lord Jesus, as Judas did. When our love for Him is real, we'll be eager to please Him in all that we think, and say, and do.

TODAY'S THOUGHT:

> Is your heart big with love for the Lord Jesus and love for others? If so, you will be a blessing to all who know you and a joy to Him.

READ ROMANS 12:14-21.

Let God Pay Back

When someone hits me, I feel like hitting back, don't you? When someone is mean to me, I feel like paying him back, with a little extra for good measure! When a boy or girl I don't like gets into trouble, I feel like saying, "Serves you right." But if I'm a Christian, I am not to do what I feel like. I must do what my King wants me to do, and He has given me some very clear rules. How am I to treat those who are unkind to me? I am to help them in every way, and pray for them—*never* to pay them back. God will punish wrongdoing, so I must leave all that to Him (v. 19). And I must try very hard to be friends with everyone (v. 18). That's the best way to come out on top. First thing you know your "enemy" will be ashamed (those kind acts of yours burning him!), and will want to make friends.

GOOD ADVICE FOR TODAY:

So far as it depends on you, try to be friends with everyone.—Romans 12:18, Laubach, *Inspired Letters*

Pay Your Debt

Debt? Perhaps you say, "I don't owe anyone anything." Oh, yes, you do! I hope you don't owe money or other things like that, but there's one thing that you owe your friends, your neighbors, even those who don't like you. You owe them *love*. If I love my neighbor as much as I love myself—if I'm honest I'll admit that I am *quite* fond of myself—I won't steal from him, lie to him, or hurt him in any way. If I live by this one rule of love, I don't need any more rules, not even the Ten Commandments. And if I'm not living by this law of love I'd better hurry and start, because my chances may soon be over. When Jesus comes the night of this life will end. It will be day then, a day that will never end. Let's get ready for it by buckling on the "armor of light." What is the armor of light? It is Jesus Himself, as verse 14 tells us.

POEM FOR TODAY:

> Dear Lord, I never can repay
> The debt of love I owe
> To You, for dying on the cross,

And suffering such pain and loss,
Because You loved me so.
So take me, Lord, and let me pay,
A little of it every day.
Let me God's love to others show,
They they may learn His love to know.

—M. L. M.

READ ROMANS 14:7-12.

What about John?

One day the Lord Jesus cornered Peter and asked him some questions about himself that made him feel very uncomfortable. When Jesus had finished talking with him He said to Peter, "Follow me." But Peter turned around and saw John, and he couldn't keep from saying, "What about John? What do you want *him* to do?" Now what John did was entirely between himself and Jesus, so Jesus had to say to Peter, "That's not your business, Peter. You follow me!" Peter learned that day what Paul is saying in our portion today. If we are Christians, we belong to Jesus and He is our Lord. Some day we shall kneel before Him and tell Him what we've done, and why. He will not ask us what our brother Bill or our sister Mary has done. So let's stop finding fault with them, and be sure that we shall not be ashamed when we stand before Him.

A BIBLE VERSE FOR TODAY:

> Little children, abide in him; that, when he shall appear, we...may not be ashamed before him.—I John 2:28

First!

Someone had said, "Let's take turns." At once every voice shouted "First." Then the voices became angry and ugly as each one insisted he said "First" first. Some began to walk away in a huff; if they couldn't be first, they wouldn't play. Is that the way Christians should act? Certainly not! Paul says we should not aim to please ourselves, but to please the other fellow. Not "me first," but "you first, me next." We should try to think up ways we can help our friends to be better Christians, and as we seek to help others, we'll become better Christians ourselves. And Paul prays (vv. 5 and 6) that the Christians in Rome will not quarrel. When two violins are tuned right, they play in harmony and make lovely music. So when we live in peace and harmony with one another, our lives are like a song of praise to God.

How to have joy: J esus (first)
O thers (next)
Y ou (last)

I Corinthians

Paul was in Ephesus when he wrote I Corinthians to the church in Corinth. He was the one who first brought the Gospel to them (see Acts 18), so of course he loved every one of them and longed to see them growing up to be strong, faithful believers in Jesus. He wanted to go back and visit them, and so he wrote to tell them he was coming. He had heard that things weren't going too well there, and he wanted to give the members a chance to put matters right before he arrived.

Let's look at a few pages of this long letter.

Saints in Sweat Shirts and Jeans

Most people think a saint is a stone statue of someone who has been dead a long time. No, if you are a Christian, you are supposed to be a saint. What—me a saint? Paul says in verse two that *every* Christian is called by God to be a saint. That doesn't mean you have to be a sort of angel-face. Real boys and he-men can be saints, because a saint is a Christian who is like his Lord, strong to do what is right no matter what the cost. If we don't have what it takes, all we need to do is *ask,* and God will give it to us. The grace which Paul writes about in verses 3 and 4 is a gift. You may have everything you need so that you can be a true saint. Love, courage, joy, peace—these are the true riches Paul is talking about in verse 5. You can have them for the asking.

A QUESTION TO ASK YOURSELF:
Am I worthy of being called a "saint"?

READ I CORINTHIANS 1:26-31.

Nothing to Brag About

When the Lord Jesus came down from Heaven to this earth, He didn't come as a king. He didn't live in a palace. He wasn't a doctor, lawyer, or professor. No, He was the son of a carpenter, born in a manger. He loved the simple things, the lilies growing in the field, the sparrows, fishermen, children. That is probably why He chose me, for I have nothing to brag about. Most of my Christian friends are simple people too. We're really just nobodies, but look what He has given us (v. 30): we're not wise, but He gives us His wisdom; we're not righteous, but He gives us His righteousness; we're not holy, but He gives us His holiness; we were slaves of sin, but He redeemed us. So we can boast about *Him,* can't we!

A HYMN FOR TODAY:

> Fairest Lord Jesus, Ruler of all nature,
> O Thou of God and man the Son,
> Thee will I cherish, Thee will I honor,
> Thou my soul's glory, joy and crown.

READ I CORINTHIANS 2:1-5.

When Paul Shook in His Shoes

Paul was a well-educated man. He had been taught by one of the cleverest teachers of those days (Acts 22:3). He was a very courageous man too, as you will remember from reading the story of his life in the Book of Acts. And yet here he tells the Corinthian Christians that when he first came to preach to them he felt so weak and so afraid that he shook all over. Why so? I think the great apostle was afraid that he might not make the Gospel message clear enough. He longed to see people saved, so he preached the simple message of Jesus and His death for us on the cross. No solos, no pictures, no refreshments, no beautiful sermon; just the straight and simple Gospel story. And He had the joy of seeing one after another saved, not because of his fine preaching, but through God's power.

TODAY'S THOUGHT:

> It is God's power that saves people and changes lives, not our cleverness or our fine words.

Read I Corinthians 3:9-15.

A Gold House or a Straw House?

It's nice to have lovely rooms, but unless your house has a good solid foundation it may come tumbling down the first time a strong wind blows. Paul tells us here that it's no use trying to build a fine life without a firm foundation. When we believe in the Lord Jesus as our Saviour, we have laid a firm foundation for our lives. Then when the storms come and the winds of trouble blow on us, we shall not go all to pieces. But what are you building on top of the foundation? Living to please ourselves is like building with straw. Living a life of usefulness and unselfishness is like building with gold and silver. Some day God's fire will test our building. It will not be completely destroyed if the foundation is there, but it will be sad if all the rest goes up in smoke. So let us ask God to help us today and every day to build with gold, silver, precious stones, so that we may win a reward.

THOUGHT FOR TODAY:

The wise man built his house upon the Rock. Are you that wise man?

READ I CORINTHIANS 9:24-27.

Out to Win

What is more thrilling than a race? The runners stand on the starting line, leaning forward, listening for the signal, their eyes on the goal ahead. The very second the gun goes off they are away like lightning, forcing every muscle, their eyes never leaving the goal for an instant. Each runner is out to win. Paul says the Christian life is a race, and Heaven is the goal. There are crowns to win—not the wreath of leaves given to the Greek runner, but a crown that will never fade. Athletes can't do just as they please, but must keep in training and obey the rules; otherwise they may be disqualified. Paul didn't want that to happen to him. If you want to win a crown you must keep going straight ahead with your eye on the goal.

A BIBLE VERSE FOR TODAY:

Let us keep on running with all our might the race God gave us to run.—Hebrews 12:1, Laubach, *Inspired Letters*

READ I CORINTHIANS 10:1-6.

Danger, Keep Off!

High voltage wires are always fenced around with barbed wire, and clear signs read: Danger, Keep Off. Suppose I am curious and I pay no attention to the sign and climb the fence. What would happen? Exactly what happened to the curious cat! If we have any sense at all, when we see a red light or a danger sign, we obey the warning. And God has a warning for us today in His Word. Paul reminds the Corinthians (and you and me) that the people of Israel all had the same chance to live in a way that was pleasing to God; but many of them loved their sinful ways more than they loved God, and God was *not pleased* with them. When God is not pleased with us, trouble is bound to follow. What happened to them should be a warning to us to stay away from sin.

> Yield not to temptation, for yielding is sin;
> Each victory will help you some other to win;
> Fight manfully onward, dark passions subdue;
> Look ever to Jesus, He'll carry you through.

31

A Way to Escape

Did you know that grumbling is a sin? We're warned about that in this chapter (v. 10). Wendell and I were talking about a wrong thing that many people do who don't know the Lord. "*I* would *never* do that," he said. I told him he'd have to keep looking to Jesus or he might sometime be too weak to say "No." We talked about Peter, who felt so strong that he said he'd gladly die for Jesus, and then just a little later swore that he never knew Him. So we all need to watch and pray (v. 12). When you did that wrong thing today did you say, "I couldn't help it"? That's not true. You can always look to Jesus for strength to overcome temptation. He has promised that no temptation will be too strong for us. If you live by verse 31 and do every single thing to please God, you'll not fall into Satan's traps.

LET'S SING:

> Ask the Saviour to help you,
> Comfort, strengthen and keep you;
> He is willing to aid you,
> He will carry you through.

READ I CORINTHIANS 12:14-18, 26-31.

There's a Job for You

Suppose your ear said to your eye, "I'm more important than you. You can't hear a thing; you can't—" How stupid! It takes many different parts, each doing its job well, to make a strong, healthy body. And all those who belong to Christ are like one body. No one can boast that he is more important than the others. We need each other. Some are like eyes and ears. They are leaders like your minister and your Sunday school teachers; others just help in small ways, like your little finger. I stood on the deck of a great ocean liner and watched while we slowly got clear of the wharf and headed out to sea. And who do you suppose turned that ship? The captain? the engines? No, two little black tugboats, puffing and pulling, way down below the deck of the big liner.

TODAY'S THOUGHT:

God needs those who are willing just to be "helps" (v. 28). Remember, there's a job for you.

READ I CORINTHIANS 13:1-6, 13.

The Valentine Chapter

Read the whole of this wonderful chapter. Try to read it in a translation which uses modern English words. Be sure to change "charity" to "love," because that's what it means. Have you heard the story of the contest between the sun and the wind? The wind bragged that he was much stronger than the sun.

"See that man walking down a country road? I could tear the coat off him in no time at all," boasted the wind. So he huffed and he puffed and he got himself into a terrible rage. But the harder he tugged at the coat, the closer the man drew it around him.

Then the sun shone out, warm and gentle, and very soon the man removed his coat. Love is like the sun—gentle, patient, kind, but stronger than hate, or jealousy, or anger. Without real love for God and love for others, our lives are useless no matter how clever we are.

> Love is so patient and so kind; Love never boils with jealousy; It never boasts, is never puffed with pride.—I Corinthians 13:4, Williams' Translation

The A B C of the Gospel

Aren't you glad the Gospel is so simple? It is explained here very clearly; no one could possibly miss it. A) Christ died for our sins—for yours, for mine. B) He was buried. There was no doubt about it; He was really dead, and they put His cold body in the grave. C) He rose on the third day. Now there are thousands of people who believe that He lived and died, but they won't believe He rose again, even though we can prove it. See how many people there are who saw Him after He rose. Count them up in verses 5—8. Paul says he saw the Lord Jesus, too. You will remember reading about that in the Book of Acts (9:3, 4). And Matthew, Mark, Luke, John and Peter all tell about His resurrection. Yes, He died for our sins and rose again. Simple, but wonderful!

(To the tune of "Jesus Loves Me")
'Tis as clear as ABC,
Jesus died for you and me;
Rose again that we might live;
All my heart to Him I give.

—M. L. M.

READ I CORINTHIANS 15:12-19.

A Huge Mistake?

Just suppose for a minute that Jesus didn't rise from the dead, and that the Easter story were a huge mistake. It is too awful to think about, but we'll mention a few things that would be true if Jesus were still in the grave. First, all the preachers in the world would be liars. Second, our faith in the Lord Jesus would amount to nothing, because a dead person couldn't help us. Third, we would still have our burden of sin. Fourth, we would die like animals, with no hope of ever rising again. No hope, no hope. How miserable we would be! So you see how important it is to believe that Jesus rose. It is like the foundation of the Empire State building. Take away that foundation, and the whole building falls to pieces like a card house.

WHEN YOU PRAY:

Thank God with all your heart that Jesus rose from the dead, and is our living Saviour.

No More Death

Death is an enemy that we can't catch and conquer. He takes away our loved ones and our friends. Doctors and nurses work so hard to rescue them, and for a time they may keep death away. But sooner or later he wins and we have to say good-by to our dear ones. But if we are Christians, we know it is not good-by for good. We know that because Jesus rose from the dead, He will one day bring back to life again all who have died. Verse 20 is like a shout of victory. Christ is risen! And His resurrection is the proof of ours, just as the first fruit that appears in summer is a promise of the harvest to come. Yes, death is an enemy, and a strong one; but Jesus is stronger, and one day He will conquer death.

A BIBLE VERSE FOR TODAY:

> And there shall be no more death, neither sorrow, nor crying, neither shall there be any more pain: for the former things are passed away.—Revelation 21:4

READ I CORINTHIANS 15:35-38, 42-44.

From Death to Life

Someone gave me some bulbs. They certainly weren't a pretty sight, twisted, brown, dirty. But I buried them in the soft earth, and soon forgot about them. Then one day I had such a lovely surprise. Here and there in my garden were the most gorgeous flowers. Then I remembered planting the bulbs. What a miracle that such a beautiful thing could come from an ugly little bulb! And you can see miracles all around in the gardens every spring and summer. Gay flowers nodding their heads because someone dug a little hole and planted a tiny, wizened seed. You wonder what kind of bodies we'll have when we're raised from the grave some day? The dead body is only the bulb or seed. We can't imagine how beautiful the new body will be. It's a miracle, just like the miracles in your garden, only much more wonderful.

POEM FOR TODAY:

Jesus arose, and we shall rise too.
Why should this seem so strange to you?
The caterpillar didn't die;
It was changed into a butterfly.

The seeds in the warm earth didn't rot,
Flowers grew up in my garden plot.
We too shall rise at God's command,
Changed by the touch of His mighty
  Hand!

—M. L. M.

In a Twinkling

Those who die believing in the Lord Jesus will rise again in beautiful new bodies, bodies fit to live in the heavenly Home with Him. What great comfort this brings to us! But even better yet is what Paul tells us here: we shall not all die. Some will be alive when Jesus comes back to earth, but we can't go to Heaven in these bodies which get tired and sick and old. God has that all taken care of, though, and Paul lets us in on a wonderful secret. *We shall all be changed.* How long will it take to give you a new body? As long as it takes you to blink your eye. What kind of body will it be? One like our Lord Jesus had when He rose from the dead. The Bible says "we shall be like him" (I John 3:2). So death can't win. Jesus is the Conqueror!

TODAY'S THOUGHT:

> Since we know [if we are saved] that we shall live *with* Jesus some day, it will pay us to live *for* Him now.

II Corinthians

Paul waited eagerly at Ephesus for an answer to his first letter to the Corinthian Church. He hoped they had paid attention to what he had told them in it, because many things needed to be put right. After a while he got tired of waiting for an answer and sent a helper of his, called Titus, to visit the church and bring back word of how things were going. But before Titus returned, Paul had to leave Ephesus in a hurry (Acts 20:1). So off he went in search of Titus, and finally met him on his way back. He was so glad to hear that his first letter had been a real blessing to the Corinthian Christians, and he sat down right away to write to them again. Let us read a little of this second letter.

READ II CORINTHIANS 1:1-5.

Where to Go in Trouble

Life isn't all sunshine and roses. We are not very old before we find out that everyone has troubles of one kind or another. Even Christians have troubles, plenty of them sometimes. Jesus didn't promise us an easy journey. He said those who follow Him would often find the going rough. Paul's life was full of dangers and difficulties, wasn't it? What's the use of being a Christian, then? Because Christians don't travel alone. We have the same kind of troubles that other people have, but close beside us walks the Lord Himself, to comfort and cheer us. He is the "God of all comfort." I couldn't face life's hard places without Him, could you? And He comforts us not only because He is our Father who loves us so much, but because He wants us to pass His comfort on to others who are in trouble.

SONG FOR TODAY:

> Jesus knows all about our struggles,
> He will guide till the day is done;
> There's not a Friend like the lowly Jesus,
> No, not one! no, not one!

READ II CORINTHIANS 2:14-17.

On Parade

Christians may have plenty of troubles, but we need never be beaten. We are followers of the King of kings, and He is the mighty Conqueror. Paul says we're marching in a parade with Him. In Bible days when a conqueror had a parade, a lot of sweet incense was burned. Our lives should be so true-blue for Jesus that they are like the sweet-smelling incense, making people want to come closer to us and find out what makes us so pleasant. If some don't like us, it is because they are like dead people who can't see, or hear, or feel. They don't know the Lord, and so they can't understand us. But remember, our lives will be like sweet perfume only if we are sincere (vv. 15, 16), as good through-and-through as we seem to be; just as nice in our homes as we are at Sunday school.

TODAY'S THOUGHT:

Jesus is never defeated, and He does not want us to be defeated either. He wants to give us victory over every bad habit and every temptation.

43

READ II CORINTHIANS 4:1-6.

Don't Lose Heart

Over and over again things happened to discourage Paul, but he spoke the truth when he said, "We do not lose heart." There were two reasons why he didn't give up. First, his conscience was clean. No matter what anyone said against him, he knew it was not true. In verse 2 he says he turned his back on everything that was not perfectly honest, and he always spoke the plain truth. The second thing that kept Paul from losing heart was this: he knew he was God's servant, speaking God's message (v. 5). When the earth was created, God made light when there was nothing but darkness; it was the same God who had shined into Paul's heart, chasing out all the darkness of sin. If He could do that for Paul, he could do it for others, even though Satan tried hard to keep them blind.

CHORUS FOR TODAY:

Come to the Light, 'tis shining for thee;
Sweetly the Light has dawned upon me;
Once I was blind, but now I can see;
The Light of the world is Jesus.

READ II CORINTHIANS 4:7-10, 16-18.

Hidden Treasure

Paul had probably seen his father and mother hiding their money and other costly treasures in a common little clay jar. They had no banks in those days, and so that was their only way of keeping things safe. In our last reading Paul spoke of the glorious light of Jesus which shines into our hearts, bringing forgiveness and love and peace. Now he says these bodies of ours are like the clay jar holding this wonderful treasure. Some day the jar will break, but that's all right; there will be a better jar to hold it. Paul was near death again and again, but within his poor, suffering body he had the life of Jesus. And he knew that all his troubles would someday be gone, but he himself would live for ever and ever with Jesus. That's why he never lost heart.

A BIBLE VERSE FOR TODAY:

> But I am keeping this jewel in an earthen jar, to prove that its surpassing power is God's, not mine.—II Corinthians 4:7, Williams' Translation

45

READ II CORINTHIANS 5:6-10.

At Home with the Lord

"Present with the Lord" (v. 8) means "at home with the Lord." What a beautiful way to speak about death! Who would be afraid of death when it means going Home, Home to be with Jesus, seeing Him face to face, talking with Him. Paul says he would far rather be there than here. Death is only the door to our heavenly Home. That's why Paul was never afraid of anything, even when he thought he might have to die (v. 6). Remember how he sang when he was in the jail at Philippi and how brave he was during that terrible storm when it seemed certain that the ship would sink? The only thing he cared about was that he might please his Lord. He knew that someday he would stand before Him, and he didn't want to feel ashamed of anything he had done.

MOTTO FOR TODAY:

My constant ambition [is] to please him.
—II Corinthians 5:9, Williams' Translation

"Things Are Different Now"

Yes, "something happened to me when I gave my heart to Jesus." Something happened to Paul, too. How about you? Remember how you used to live entirely for yourself? You wanted the biggest piece of pie, the best apple, first place in all the games? Now you are eager to please your Lord and Saviour; you try to be kind to those who are not too kind to you; you are ready to let the other fellow go first. What's happened? The old "you" has gone into the grave with Jesus; and a new "you" has risen with Him. Before, you didn't want to be good, and your parents and teachers had a bad time with you. It's quite different now, not because someone has told you to "be good or else," but because you *love* the Christ who died for you, and He has made you *new*.

A Chorus for Today:

> I'll live for Him who died for me,
> How happy then my life shall be!
> I'll live for Him who died for me,
> My Saviour and my God!

READ II CORINTHIANS 6:4-7.

The Christian's Armor

Did you know that the word "minister" (v. 4) means servant? In so many different ways Paul proved that he was a faithful servant of the Lord Jesus. See what he suffered—beatings, prison, hunger, sleepless nights (watchings). Many different kinds of hardship he bore patiently. You and I won't likely have to go through things like that. How then can we prove that we, too, are faithful servants? Verses 6 and 7 are for us. Notice two things especially: 1) God's servants must *always* speak the truth; 2) God's servants must be completely protected by the armor of righteousness. What is this armor of righteousness? Clean, honest, right living, so that when Satan shoots his darts and cries, "Liar, cheat, troublemaker," they just can't hurt us. Paul wore that armor (Acts 24:16). Do you?

A HYMN FOR TODAY:

> Stand up, stand up for Jesus—
> Stand in His strength alone;
> The arm of flesh will fail you—
> Ye dare not trust your own;

Put on the gospel armor,
And watching unto prayer,
Where duty calls, or danger,
Be never wanting there.

READ II CORINTHIANS 9:6-8, 15.

Do It Generously and Joyfully

I was busy getting ready for Sunday school when my little boy came to me with his hands full of pennies. "Look, Mummy, they're all mine."

"Oh my!" I exclaimed. "How many are you going to give to Jesus?"

In a second the sunshine was gone from his face, and he hung his head as he muttered miserably, "I'm not going to give mine; I'm going to give Daddy's."

Slowly and sadly he went back to his room. But after a while he came quietly back to the kitchen and tugged at my skirt.

"See," he said, and his eyes were shining now. In his hand were six pennies. "Mine—for Jesus."

I was in his department that morning when he marched up and put his very own gift in the tiny tin church. There wasn't a happier boy anywhere in all the world. And the Lord was happy too, because He loves a cheerful giver. He Himself has given us "far more than words can describe" (v. 15, Laubach).

THOUGHT FOR TODAY:

"God loveth a cheerful giver."—II Corinthians 9:7

Galatians

In Acts 16:6 we read that Paul preached the Gospel in Galatia. This was a province in Asia Minor; look for it on your map. Many Galatians believed in the Lord Jesus, and started little churches here and there. Soon after Paul left, some teachers came to those new believers and taught them things that were not true. Paul was very distressed to hear about this, and so he wrote a letter to the Galatian Christians. God told Paul what to write, and He meant the letter to help us, too, as well as the Galatians. So now it is one of the books of our precious Bible.

READ GALATIANS 1:1-8.

Only One Gospel

These Galatian Christians were like the butterflies who flit from flower to flower. When they found something good they wanted it, but in a little while they were off to try out something else. When Paul brought them the good news of a Saviour, they believed and were so happy. But soon a man came along who pretended to be very wise. He told them that it was not enough just to believe in the Lord Jesus as their Saviour. They must *do* certain things in order to be saved. Paul tells them in this letter that there is only one Gospel, and in these verses you have just read, he explains what the Gospel message is: the Lord Jesus died for our sins, and rose from the dead (vv. 4 and 1), that we might have God's wonderful peace in our hearts.

A WORD OF WARNING:

> God's Word tells us very plainly how to be saved. Never listen to anyone who tries to tell you there is another way.

READ GALATIANS 1:11-17.

You Can't Work Your Way

The word Gospel means good news. What's good about it? That although I cannot keep God's law in my own strength, I can come to Him and receive forgiveness for all my sins. Why? Because Jesus took my place and died for me. That's really good news, isn't it! And Paul says he didn't make that up, neither did any other man. That's God's good news. Until God made this clear to Paul, he did everything he possibly could to try to please God and work his way to Heaven. But it just can't be done. Paul says it is all "by his grace" (v. 15), and "grace" means a *gift*. Have you accepted God's gift, the Lord Jesus Christ?

A BIBLE VERSE FOR TODAY:

> By grace are ye saved through faith, . . .
> not of works, lest any man [boy or girl]
> should boast.—Ephesians 2:8, 9

Obey or Die!

Perhaps you are one of those who do the best they can to keep God's laws. You wouldn't think of stealing—nothing like that. Lie? Oh! just a little one sometimes. Disobey? Now and then. Wait a minute! Do you know that one "little" sin makes you a lawbreaker? There are no little sins in God's sight. One sin makes you a sinner; and "the soul that sinneth it shall die" (Ezek. 18: 4). So it's really no use at all trying to work your way to Heaven, as we saw in our last reading. What then? Praise God, He sent His dear Son to bear the penalty for my sin and yours. Do you believe that? If you do, that's faith. When you believe that Jesus died in your place, God writes, "Not guilty," across the record of your life.

A CHORUS FOR TODAY:

> I do believe, I now believe,
> That Jesus died for me;
> And by His blood, His precious blood,
> I am from sin set free.

Adopted

If you are an adopted child there is one difference between you and other boys and girls. Your mother and father didn't *have* to have you for a son or daughter. They loved you so much and wanted you so badly that they were willing to do almost anything to have you. God didn't have to have us in His family. We were all sinners; we didn't love Him, nor even know Him. But He loved us so much He sent His only Son to die for us. And all those who trust in the Lord Jesus as Saviour are adopted into His family. We are no longer servants of Satan; we are sons and daughters of God. Tenderly He says to us, "My son, My daughter," and with hearts overflowing with love we look into His face and say, "My Father." Yes, I'm a child of the King!

A HYMN FOR TODAY:

> I once was an outcast stranger on earth,
> A sinner by name, and an alien by birth.
> But I've been adopted; my name's written down,
> An heir to a mansion, a robe and a crown.

READ GALATIANS 5:13-18.

Do You Bite?

Of course you wouldn't think of biting any-one! But wait a minute. Paul is writing this let-ter to Christians, and he says if you bite one an-other, watch out, you may end by eating each other up! Using your teeth on someone is not the only way to bite. We can bite with bitter, unkind words. But that's not how an adopted child of God should act. It's true that Jesus has set us free from the chains of sin, but we're not free to do as we please. Like our Father, we should love others so much that we'll be glad to serve them. But, you say, sometimes I just can't do what I know is right. You're learning an im-portant lesson. God's Holy Spirit wants to lead you every moment of every day. What you can't do by yourself, He will give you strength to do. But you must learn to listen to His voice, and obey.

A BIBLE VERSE TO MEMORIZE:

By love serve one another.—Galatians 5:13

READ GALATIANS 5:22-26.

God's Trees

What horrible, rotten fruit we may bear when left to ourselves! The ugly list is found in verses 20 and 21. God's trees bear beautiful fruit. I want this fruit in my life, don't you? I want to be loving, joyful, peaceful, patient, kind, good, faithful, gentle. How can I have this fruit? By trying very, very hard? No, that's hopeless. Our reading says these lovely things are the "fruit of the Spirit." When I allow God's Spirit to live within me, when I obey Him instead of taking my own way, these beautiful things appear in my life, like good fruit on a healthy tree. And the more good fruit there is, the less room for ugly fruit like pride, envy, anger, quarreling. But remember, the lovely fruit Paul describes here is the fruit of the Holy Spirit living within us. When we have this fruit, people will know we are Christians because we are like the Lord Jesus.

O blessed Holy Spirit,
Live out Thy life in me.
I want to be like Jesus,
From sin and self set free.

—M. L. M.

READ GALATIANS 6:1-5.

Don't Fool Yourself

You know that boy who is always getting into trouble? You probably think he's awful and you wouldn't be like him for anything. But why aren't you like him? Because you're such a wonderful boy or girl? No, indeed! If someone hadn't told you about the Lord Jesus, helped you to give your heart to Him, taken you to Sunday school and church, you might be just like that other fellow. If you think you're *somebody* you're fooling yourself. That's what God says in verse 3. And if you don't watch out and pray earnestly, you may find temptation too strong for you. So instead of talking about the other fellow, be kind to him and try to help him to be better. Then you'll be carrying out Christ's law, the law of love.

SOMETHING TO THINK ABOUT:

> When we do wrong, we often excuse ourselves, but we hardly ever excuse others. Is that fair?

READ GALATIANS 6:7-10.

You Can't Fool God

We may fool others; we may fool ourselves; but we can't fool God. Did you ever sow an onion? What came up—a rose? Of course not! We reap exactly what we sow. We may pretend we are very nice, and that we are sowing seeds of love and kindness, but if we're sowing weed seeds of meanness, hate, jealousy, disobedience, we're going to reap a harvest of trouble. If we sow good seeds of kindness, love, unselfishness, obedience, we shall reap not only all those lovely things, but we shall also reap *everlasting life*. When you sow your flower seeds in the spring, do you find the flowers blooming the very next day? No, gardeners have to be patient and wait for the harvest. And we must be patient too, willing to sow the good seeds day by day, willing to wait for the harvest.

A HYMN FOR TODAY:

Sowing in the morning, sowing seeds of
kindness,
Sowing in the noontide and the dewy eve;

Waiting for the harvest, and the time of
    reaping,
We shall come rejoicing, bringing in the
    sheaves.

Letters from a Prisoner

If you got a letter from a friend who had been in jail for years for no fault of his own, you would expect a very blue letter, full of complaints, wouldn't you? Paul wrote several long letters when he was a prisoner at Caesarea (Acts 24:27) and Rome (Acts 28:16, 30), and we shall now read parts of three of these prison letters: Ephesians (to the church at Ephesus), Philippians (to the church at Philippi), and Colossians (to the church at Colosse). But don't think for a minute that we'll be reading sad letters. Just the opposite! The letters seem to be written by a man who is bubbling over with joy. Paul had learned the secret of joy even though there was nothing you could see to make him happy. The happiness was deep down in his heart, and happenings couldn't change it. So now I'm eager to read these letters, aren't you?

Ephesians

Although Paul was in jail he didn't waste any time feeling sorry for himself. He was always thinking of the people near and far-off whom he had brought to the Lord, and he spent long hours writing these wonderful letters to them. This one is addressed to the Christians in Ephesus. We read about Paul's missionary work in that city in Acts 19. I counted and found that he mentions "Heaven" or "heavenly places" six times in the first three chapters. Can you realize what a comfort it was to Paul to think of Heaven, when he was a prisoner in chains? Though his body was chained to a Roman soldier, his spirit was happy and free, having sweet talks with his Lord in "heavenly places." Let's read parts of this letter.

Chosen

Blessings? More than we can count! The first wonderful blessing is that we Christians were chosen by God long, long before we were born, even before there was a world. But, you say, you chose *Him* when you became a Christian. That's true; but you see, as Paul says here, long before you chose Him, He knew you would do that and in His great love and mercy He chose *you*. He opened His arms wide, and you ran into them. How safe and happy that makes me feel! And that's not all. Way back there before the world began He loved you and me and planned to adopt us. Then He sent His own dear Son to die that we might be redeemed, bought back from Satan and forgiven. We didn't deserve it, did we? That's what Paul means when He says it's all because of the "riches of his grace."

SOMETHING TO THANK GOD FOR:

If you are saved, you are chosen, redeemed, forgiven, adopted.

READ EPHESIANS 1:15-21.

The Greatest Name in the World

Name the greatest man that ever lived, a name known to nearly every living person. Washington? Lincoln? There is a name far greater than these, much greater than anyone who has ever lived, or will yet live. It is the name of Jesus. Paul says that God's mighty power raised Him from the dead, up, up, above all rulers, kings, presidents. Yes, Jesus is greater than them all. But the most wonderful thing about it is that He is *my* Saviour and Friend. And the same mighty power that raised Jesus from the dead is working in me and for me. Isn't it wonderful to be a Christian, to know this great Jesus as our Friend, and to look forward to being with Him in Heaven some day?

A POEM FOR TODAY:

Greater than all, far greater than all,
Jesus my Lord is high above all.
Wonder of wonders, He loves even me,
Left Heaven's glory my Saviour to be!

—M. L. M.

READ EPHESIANS 2:4-9.

Rich Beyond Words

My heavenly Father is "rich beyond words." That's exactly what verse 7 means. He has huge storehouses of grace. What is grace? Grace is a free gift, something you didn't earn. Our heavenly Father has so many of these gifts for you and me that we couldn't begin to name them all. The first of these is His gift of salvation. How did we get it? Simply by believing His Word, by *faith*. But He Himself gave us the faith we needed. So there isn't a thing to boast about, is there? Especially not when we remember what we were before we were saved. We were like dead people. We couldn't see or hear or feel the things that really matter, like God, His Word, peace, joy, eternal life. How glad I am to be alive now because of God's great goodness to me!

A POEM FOR TODAY:

> I would not work my soul to save,
> That work my Lord has done.
> But I would work like any slave,
> For love of God's dear Son.

READ EPHESIANS 3:14-21.

Can God?

"Can God climb up a blade of grass, Granny?" My little boy's question made Granny smile.

"That's a funny question to ask, Wendell," she answered.

"But He *can,* can't He, Granny; because God can do everything."

"Oh yes," said Granny, "but He wouldn't want to do that."

It is quite true that God is able to do everything. Yes, much, much more than you would ever ask Him to do, even far more than you think He can (v. 20). But He won't use His wonderful power to do useless things, or to satisfy our greediness. He will use His power to make us strong, brave followers of Jesus (v. 16). And when we become citizens of Heaven and belong to God's family (v. 15), Jesus lives within us and fills us to overflowing with His great love.

TRY THIS:

> When Satan knocks at your heart, ask Jesus to go to the door. Remember, He lives within you if you are His child.

READ EPHESIANS 4:1-6.

Scout's Honor

If you are, or ever were a Scout, you'll know that every Scout is expected to live up to certain high standards of conduct. You were not accepted until you knew just what was expected of you, and after that you wouldn't dream of doing anything to bring dishonor on the name of Scout. We Christians have some very high rules of conduct too, and in the verses you have just read, Paul begs the Ephesian Christians—and you and me— to live up to our wonderful name of Christian. The Lord expects His followers to be humble and gentle, patient and loving with one another (v. 2). We should try very hard (endeavor) to keep out of quarrels and to live peacefully with other Christians, because we all belong to one family. We have one Father and one Lord Jesus, and we have the same bright hope of being with Him in Heaven some day.

WHEN YOU PRAY:

Ask the Lord to help you today that everything you say and do may be worthy of the name of Christian—Christ's man, woman, boy or girl.

Read Ephesians 4:25-28.

No Room for Satan

Are you a Christian? Then Jesus lives in your heart. But how many rooms have you given Him? He doesn't want only a little apartment in your heart; He wants *all* of you. And if you don't give Him all, then Satan will be happy to take what's left. The unhappiest person in the world is the Christian who is letting Satan have a little place in his heart and life. That's why Paul says, "Don't give the Devil a chance" (see v. 27). So when he tempts you to lie, don't listen to him, but whisper a quick prayer to Jesus. There is a kind of anger *against* sin that is not wrong, but it is a safe rule for you and me never to let Satan stir us up to be angry. If you have listened to Satan and become angry with someone, be sure to make up before night comes, because you might never have the chance to settle that quarrel.

TODAY'S WARNING:

"You must not give the Devil a chance."
—Laubach. Don't listen to him for a moment or let him have the tiniest corner in your heart.

Keep Your Mouth Clean

I'm not telling you to clean your teeth and rinse your mouth, though that is important! There is something much more important than that. A boy or girl is said to have a "dirty mouth" when he speaks words that are not clean and pure. Sometimes people have mean mouths, speaking unkind, bitter words. It's really all a matter of what is in our hearts. Our mouths are like a fountain, sending out what bubbles up from deep down in our hearts. That's why Paul tells us in our portion today to be "tender-hearted," loving and forgiving others. Then our mouths will speak only clean, pure, kind words, words that will bring joy and not pain to the blessed Holy Spirit who lives within us (v. 30).

A PRAYER FOR TODAY:

Set a watch, O Lord, before my mouth;
keep the door of my lips.—Psalm 141:3.

Children of Light

"Once it was all dark within you" (v. 8, Laubach). Yes, that was before Jesus came into your heart; but now that He lives within you, there is sunshine and gladness, for He is the light of the world. Nothing grows well in the dark, nothing except spiders and beetles and other "creepy" things. My plants die if I leave them in a damp, dark corner of the cellar; but when I place them in the sunlight they grow strong and healthy. And when Jesus shines into our hearts we begin to grow good fruits, things that are good, right, and true (v. 9). So if you're really a member of God's household, one of His dear children, follow your Father's example. Be loving like your Saviour (vv. 1, 2). Please Him by acting like children of the light.

A SONG FOR TODAY:

> There's sunlight in my soul today,
> More glorious and bright
> Than glows in any earthly sky,
> For Jesus is my Light.
> Oh, there's sunshine, blessed sunshine,
> When the peaceful, happy moments roll;
> When Jesus shows His smiling face,
> There is sunshine in the soul.

71

Read Ephesians 5:15-20.

Watch Your Step

Did you ever see a cat walking along the top of a fence that was spiked with barbed wire? How carefully pussy placed each soft, furry foot lest she should hurt herself! That's how we should live as Christians in a world that doesn't love our Saviour (v. 15). We should be very careful what we do and say lest we displease the Lord and bring trouble on ourselves. And so we ought not to do foolish things, but find out what God wants us to do (v. 17). We should make good use of our time (v. 16), not doing just as we please. Satan doesn't like happy people. He likes to see grumbling, gloomy Christians. So if we make a habit of just being thankful for everything, and often singing a cheery song of praise to our wonderful Lord, Satan is not so likely to get a chance to tempt us.

TRY THIS:

> Sing, sing, sing.
> Make melody with your heart.
> Not only for the sunny days—

When things go wrong sing songs of praise,
And sing, sing, sing.
In everything give thanks.

—M. L. M.

READ EPHESIANS 6:1-7.

Good Enough

Not long ago I had to tell my Marilyn that her work was not done properly. "It's good enough, isn't it?" she asked. I insisted that the job was not finished, but she asked again, "But it's good enough, isn't it?"

Is that your motto—good enough? I think a great many people are satisfied with doing things "good enough," but that kind of work doesn't get you anywhere. If Beethoven or any of the other great musicians had been satisfied to practice just "good enough," they would never have blessed the world with their music. No, Christians are not to be "good enough" people, aiming only to make our work *look* all right. We are to do everything knowing God's eye sees everywhere. We must do every job "as to the Lord." And don't forget, God expects Christian children to be obedient and respectful to their parents. Obedient children usually become healthy, successful men and women.

HINT FOR HAPPINESS:

> Work well, even when men's eyes are not on you.—Ephesians 6:6, Laubach

READ EPHESIANS 6:10-13.

Our Tricky Enemy

"If I knew where Satan was, I'd shoot him," said my little boy one day. Young as he was, he had already found out that there is a very real "someone" who tries hard to get him to do what is wrong; and he thought it would be so nice if we could find him and put an end to him. Yes, it would, but it's not as easy as that. As long as we live we'll have to be on our guard against this Number One enemy. And he's so much stronger than we that we simply can't fight him with the strength we have. We have to have the Lord's strength. And we have to be fully armed too; not one piece of armor missing, or Satan will be sure to find that weak spot and shoot one of his poison arrows right there. What is this armor? We'll find out in our next reading.

TODAY'S HELPFUL HINT:

Never let Satan see your back. With God's help you can win the battle.

READ EPHESIANS 6:14-18.

Arrow-proof Armor

When David volunteered to fight the giant, King Saul offered him his own armor. But when David tried it on, it didn't fit. It was much too big for him. But here is a suit of armor that will fit you whether you are short or tall, old or young. Here are the pieces: 1) A belt of truth. This is a most important part of the armor. Are we truthful, *always,* so that everyone knows our word can be depended on? 2) A breastplate of right living. No amount of mere talking will do any good unless it is backed by right living. 3) Gospel shoes—being ready to go here and there telling others about Jesus. 4) A shield of faith—Satan's burning arrows just bounce off it! 5) A helmet of salvation—knowing you are saved. 6) A sword —God's Word. Then, don't forget to pray—in the morning and at night. Yes, and over and over again through the day.

A HYMN FOR TODAY:

> Sound the battle cry! See the foe is nigh;
> Raise the standard high, for the Lord;
> Gird your armor on, stand firm every one;
> Rest your cause upon His holy Word.

Philippians

This is another letter written by Paul from his prison room. It is addressed to the church at Philippi. Do you remember how that church began? We read in Acts 16 about Paul's vision in the night of a man of Macedonia begging him, "Come over and help us." And Paul answered that call and went straight to the largest city of Macedonia, which was Philippi. There, on a lovely Sabbath morning, at an open air service by the riverside, he won Lydia to Christ, and she became the first member of the church there. One by one others believed and joined. Paul loved them all, and wrote this letter to help them in their Christian life.

Happy Memories

Supposing your parents, school teacher, Sunday school teacher, or minister should write you a letter when they no longer have you with them. Could they say, and really mean it, "Everything I remember about you makes me happy and thankful to God for you"? I want to live from day to day in such a way that when I leave here, those who know me will have no sad memories of times when I have grieved them. How about you? When your mother prays for you, does she feel hurt and sad because you've been disobedient, unkind, quarrelsome? Or can she just thank God for giving her children that are always a joy to her? Of one thing you can be very sure— if you really want to please the Lord and do His will always, then He will make you the kind of person He wants you to be, not all at once, but day by day, until Jesus comes (v. 6).

WHEN YOU PRAY:

Ask God to help you live today so that when night comes no one will have any unhappy memories of you.

READ PHILIPPIANS 1:9-14.

Without Wax

A strange title, isn't it? In verse 10 Paul prays that the Philippian Christians may be *sincere*. That is an interesting word which comes from two Latin words meaning without *(sine)* wax *(cerum)*. In those days many figures were carved in stone by men called sculptors. Sometimes the sculptor was not honest, and he would fill up cracks with wax to make his statue look good. But alas! whoever bought one of these statues would find out sooner or later, because it would break apart. It was not sincere, you see. It was a sham. God wants Christians to be true-blue through and through; to have real love for Himself and one another, love that grows day by day (v. 9) ; to be like a tree covered with good fruit (v. 11). Want to know what Paul means in verses 12-14? Look up Romans 8:28. Paul let his light shine in dark places, didn't he?

LET'S SING:

> I would be true, for there are those who
> trust me.
> I would be pure, for there are those who
> care.

79

I would be strong, for there is much to
   suffer.
I would be brave, for there is much to dare.

Better Than Life

If you're young and strong, I am sure you feel that life is wonderful, and you would like it to go on forever. But remember, Paul was no longer young when he wrote these words, and he was in prison. He didn't know when he might have to suffer torture or a painful death. So he said as far as this life goes, he had only one wish—that he might never do anything for which he would afterward be ashamed. He was determined to honor his Lord, even though he had to suffer and perhaps die. He longed so much to be with Jesus in Heaven that death seemed better than life, but he was willing to stay on earth, yes, even in prison, in order that he might help those whom he had led to the Saviour.

TODAY'S THOUGHT:

Make Paul's earnest aim yours: 1) Never to do anything for which afterward you would feel ashamed. 2) To honor your Lord in everything you say and do.

READ PHILIPPIANS 1:27-30.

Stand Firm

What do you think of the boy who runs away and hides when someone threatens to beat him up, or even just laughs at him? Not much! What did Jesus do when wicked men told lies about Him, when they spit on Him and beat Him? He was not afraid; He stood firm. Instead of answering back, He prayed for those who were treating Him so shamefully. Only when we copy our dear Lord are we worthy followers of Him. "Conversation" in verse 27 means not only what we say, but how we act. And when we stand firm, quietly, bravely, it is plain to see who is right and who is wrong (v. 28). We're not to be surprised if it is not always easy to be a Christian. If it were easy we would not be strong. No, God wants us to be willing to suffer for Jesus' sake.

A BIBLE VERSE FOR TODAY:

> When any of you suffer for being a Christian, do not be ashamed. Praise God that you can suffer for the name of Christ.
> —I Peter 4:16, Laubach

Others

When the Lord Jesus does so much for us, encouraging us, loving and comforting us (v. 1), surely we ought to please Him by living at peace with one another. Paul says that if he could know that the Christians at Philippi didn't quarrel, his cup of joy would be full to the brim. (v. 2). The secret of living peacefully with one another is to think and really believe that the "other fellow" is better than yourself (v. 3). If Bill thought John was better than himself, he wouldn't be jealous when John was elected president of the young people. And John wouldn't get "stuck-up" because he was president. He would be figuring out how he could help this one and that one (v. 4). Yes, ours would be a wonderful church if we *all* had the same mind, humble, loving, thoughtful of others.

HINT FOR HAPPINESS:

Each counting other better than himself.
—Philippians 2:3, A.S.V.

READ PHILIPPIANS 2:5-11.

Change Your Mind

If you don't get along with other people, you need to change your mind. In our last reading Paul begged the Christians at Philippi to all have the same mind, so that they would have the same love one for another, and would get along together. Now he points out that this will work if they all have the mind of the Lord Jesus. What kind of mind did He have? His was certainly a humble mind. Though He was God, He came to this earth as a helpless, tiny baby, and grew up to be a servant to everyone. Then, because He loved us so much, He took our place and died on a cross of shame. We'll find it easy to get along with others if our minds are even a little like His. Do *you* need to change your mind?

A PRAYER POEM FOR TODAY:

> I would have the Saviour's mind;
> Make me loving, pure and kind;
> More like Him from day to day,
> Walking humbly in His way.

—M. L. M.

READ PHILIPPIANS 2:12-16.

Don't Live on Grumble Street

Good works do not save us. It is certainly "not by works of righteousness [right living] we have done, but according to his mercy he saved us" (Titus 3:5). But after we are saved, it is most important that we do what is right. Good works are the fruit of a true Christian, and when others can't see any change in our lives, they have a right to question whether we are really God's children. God works *in* our hearts, but we must try hard to work *out* in kind deeds all that He works *in*. Do you ever grumble? Don't! It isn't worthy of one in whose heart the Lord is working. Ever argue when you're told to do something: "Why? *She* didn't have to . . ." Does it sound familiar? It isn't what a child of God should do, and it will put your light out fast (v. 15)!

TRY THIS:

Every time you're tempted to grumble today, stop and sing a cheerful chorus.

READ PHILIPPIANS 3:13-15.

On Your Mark

If a runner wants to win the race there are some things he *must* do and some he cannot do. He must put everything he has into his running, straining every muscle to go swiftly on, keeping his eye on the finishing line. If he stops for even a minute he will get way behind. If he looks around to see how the other runners are doing, he'll lose the race. The Christian life is like a race, a race uphill. God Himself cheers us on and up. We shall reach the finishing line when our earthly life is done, but whether we get a prize or not will depend on how well we have run. Perhaps you haven't run so well up to now? Tell the Lord about it, ask His help in the race, then forget the past and run!

A VERSE OF AN OLD HYMN:

> Run the straight race through God's good
>   grace,
> Lift up thine eyes, and seek His face,
> Life with its way before us lies,
> Christ is the path, and Christ the prize.

READ PHILIPPIANS 3:17, 20, 21.

Follow the Leader

Of what country are you a citizen? Paul said he was a citizen of Heaven. (The word "conversation" in v. 20 means "country" or "citizenship.") When I took Jesus as my Saviour, I became a citizen of Heaven too, and I'm on my way to that wonderful Country where I shall be with Him. You want to go there too? First you must become a citizen by accepting the Lord Jesus as your Saviour; then follow Him each day and He will lead you safely there. He said, "I am the way" (John 14:6), the only Way to Heaven. It is also good to have your eye on some older person who follows very close to Jesus, perhaps your mother, father, minister, Sunday school teacher. Paul told the Corinthians to copy him, and we know he was a good leader to follow.

SOMETHING TO REMEMBER:

The best Christian is sometimes disappointing. Jesus never fails—keep your eyes on Him.

A Penny for Your Thoughts

Did you ever realize how very busy our minds are? Even when we are asleep they keep on working. All day long they are working away. Some people say, "My mind was a blank." But I don't think anyone's mind is ever really blank. And do you know that it matters so very much what we think about, even though no one but God knows what our thoughts are? Why? Because what we think about shows on our faces, and in what we say and do. If we think mean and ugly thoughts, we shall do mean things, and our faces will become ugly. So Paul urges us to have happy thoughts (v. 4), peaceful thoughts (vv. 6, 7), and pure thoughts (v. 8). When are we to be happy? Always! For what are we to be thankful? Everything! How? By telling God all our troubles and trusting Him to work things out for the best.

TODAY'S THOUGHT:

When our thoughts are happy, peaceful, pure, we shall be gentle and patient with everyone.

Read Philippians 4:10-13, 19.

Are You Needy or Greedy?

Do you have everything you want? No? Well, what do you want that you don't have? A new bicycle, a color television, one hundred dollars? But wait a minute. Are these things you really need? If you're honest, I think you'll admit that you have everything you need, and a whole lot more than you need. Paul had learned a most important lesson. In fact what Paul learned is a secret key that never fails to unlock the door to happiness. He had learned to be content with what he had. If God sent him plenty, his heart was full of thanks; but if he didn't have one thing more than he needed, he was thankful and contented, too. Little things made him just as happy as big things (v. 12). He refused to be miserable. He didn't worry, either, because he knew that God would give him everything he really needed (v. 19).

QUESTION FOR TODAY:

Do you own this key of contentment? Hang on to it, and you'll always be happy.

Colossians

This letter, like Ephesians and Philippians, was also written by Paul when he was a prisoner. It was sent from Rome to the city of Colosse, in the Province of Asia. You can find it on a map showing the journeys of Paul. We do not read in Acts of Paul beginning a church in Colosse, but since it was not very far from Ephesus, where he spent two years, probably some who were saved there were from Colosse, and took the Gospel to their friends when they went back home.

READ COLOSSIANS 1:9-14.

Naturalized Citizens

Perhaps you were born an American. I was not, but a few years ago I transferred my citizenship from Canada to the United States. I am what they call a naturalized citizen, and I am trying to be a good American. No one is born a citizen of Heaven, but when we trust Jesus as our Saviour, our citizenship is transferred from Satan's kingdom to God's (v. 13). I'm glad I'm no longer a citizen of Satan's "dominion of darkness" (v. 13, Williams). Paul prayed that the Colossian Christians would be worthy of their citizenship; that they would be *fully* pleasing to the Lord, busy in every kind of good work, constantly learning more about their wonderful God. We can't be worthy citizens of Heaven in our own strength, but God will give us His strength that we may always please Him in all that we do and say and think.

QUESTION FOR TODAY:

Are you a citizen of Heaven? Do you act like one at home, at school, on the playground?

91

READ COLOSSIANS 2:6-10.

How About Your Roots?

There's nothing dull about God's Word. It is full of lovely pictures, and in these few verses there are three interesting pictures of the Christian life. First, it is a walk, a day-by-day walk with God. Of course you can't walk with Him until you agree to go His way. You did that when you received Him as your Saviour. Second, the Christian life is like a tree. Did you ever see one ripped up by the roots after a storm? Short, spindly roots probably, or maybe diseased roots. If you're going to be a strong Christian, be sure to send your roots deep down into the Lord Jesus. You'll do this by reading His Word, praying and witnessing. Third, your life is like a building, so be very certain you have a good foundation. Build your life on the Lord Jesus Christ.

TODAY'S THOUGHT:

> There are those who will try to turn you aside from the teaching of God's Word, but if you're walking day by day with Him, He will keep you from all that would spoil your Christian life.

READ COLOSSIANS 3:1-4.

Dead, But Very Much Alive

Where's your heart? I mean, where are the things you love the most? Are they right here around you—the clothes you wear, the food you eat, your house, your TV? If you're a Christian your heart should be on better things, because you don't belong down here now. When Jesus died, He died in your place; when He rose from the dead, you rose too, a new person to live a new life. He went ahead to Heaven to prepare a place for you, and some day you are going to be with Him there. So you ought to be getting ready right now, and you can do so by constantly remembering where you belong. You can determine to love what Jesus loves, and do what He would do.

IS THIS TRUE OF YOU?

Things I loved before have passed away;
Things I love far more have come to stay.

READ COLOSSIANS 3:8-13.

Throw Away Your Old Clothes

When Jesus saved you, He made you brand new. You began to see how awful your old habits were, like old clothes that you would be glad to get rid of. There were those ugly things called anger, bad temper, lying, mean talk about others, dirty words and stories. You realized that a Christian has no business wearing them because they belong to your old self, and Jesus has made you a new person. No, we must wear the new clothes God has given us—kindness, humility, gentleness, patience, forgiveness. (How about that quarrel?) Nice things to read about and easy to talk about, but let's put them into our day-by-day living. Do you really want to wear these new and lovely clothes? Then you must let God's Holy Spirit have every room in your heart. He will make a new person of you.

WHEN YOU PRAY:

Ask God to take every ugly sin and habit from your life and make you like the Lord Jesus. He will give you a completely new "outfit."

94

The Secret of Happiness

In our last reading we thought about the beautiful new clothes God wants us to wear. In these verses Paul tells us about the most important piece of that clothing. If we have it, we shall have all the other things we need; if we don't have it, we won't have the other lovely clothes— no, not one piece. It is *love*. When we have love, our new outfit is complete. And of course Satan won't like to see us all decked out in our new clothes, and he will try to trip us up. The cure for that is to turn a deaf ear to anything that disturbs God's peace in our hearts, and to be always thankful to Him for everything He sends into our lives. How can we do that? By reading and memorizing His precious Word, and then by asking His help and blessing in everything we do.

A Bible Verse to Live By:

> And whatsoever ye do in word or deed, do all in the name of the Lord Jesus, giving thanks to God and the Father by him.—Colossians 3:17

Wash Those Dishes for the Lord

They say "a word to the wise is sufficient." It would surely be sufficient if we would not only hear God's Word but obey it. We read the Bible, and listen to our Sunday school teachers and our ministers. We agree that we *ought* to do what God's Word says. But doing and talking about it are two different things. Here in this passage is a word for wives, husbands, children, fathers and servants. We know just how to please the Lord, but knowing is not enough. Do you obey your parents *in all things?* Do you do your work *well,* as if the Lord Jesus were standing close by, and you were doing it for Him? If you do, then you are pleasing Him, and He will reward you. Verse 25 is not a happy note on which to end, but it's a solemn warning, meant for you and me.

A THOUGHT FOR TODAY:

> Whether you work or whether you play,
> In deed, and word, and thought,
> Do it well as unto the Lord,
> Whether you're watched or not.

I Thessalonians

In Acts 17:1-9 we read about Paul's first visit to the city of Thessalonica. It had not been easy to preach the Gospel there. Satan had stirred up a mob to try to get rid of Paul, but in spite of that, many had been saved. A few months later, when Paul was staying in Corinth, he wrote this letter and sent it back to the Christians in Thessalonica. It was the first letter that he wrote which has been kept for us as part of our Bible. It was not only a big help to those new Christians, but has blessed and helped Christians ever since. God will speak to you as you read some parts of this wonderful letter.

READ I THESSALONIANS 1:2-10.

Imitators

I knew a little girl who admired her grandfather so much that she even tried to imitate the way he chewed his food! Do you know someone you think such a lot of that you try to be like him? The Christians in Thessalonica admired and imitated Paul (v. 6). That was safe, because Paul imitated the Lord Jesus. People would not go wrong copying Him. Be sure you're copying someone who is following very close to Jesus. These Thessalonians were good imitators, because they were full of joy in knowing Jesus at the very same time they were suffering for His sake (v. 6). Paul was like that. He had to take a lot of persecution for being a Christian, but still he was "always rejoicing" (II Cor. 6:10). The Christians at Thessalonica were full of joy because they were "all-out" for Jesus. Their lives and their lips were a testimony to Him.

A QUESTION FOR TODAY:

Is anyone imitating you? Is your life a safe pattern to follow?

READ I THESSALONIANS 3:7-13.

Are You Ready?

Jesus is coming again. Paul writes of His coming at the close of every chapter of this letter. It was on his mind constantly. The thought of seeing Jesus again made Paul eager to be ready to meet Him. He longed that the people he had brought to know Jesus would be ready too. The Christians in Thessalonica had suffered a lot of persecution, and Paul worried lest they might become discouraged and think it wasn't worth being a Christian. So he had sent his helper, Timothy, to find out how they were getting along. Timothy brought back good news about them, and Paul tells them in these verses how happy that had made him. Do you bring joy to someone's heart—your parents, Sunday school teacher, minister—because you are pleasing the Lord day by day? Is your life clean, and your love for others growing stronger all the time, so that you won't be blamed for anything when Jesus comes (v. 13)?

A QUESTION FOR TODAY:

> If Jesus came today, would you be ready to meet Him joyfully?

READ I THESSALONIANS 4:9-12.

Mind Your Own Business

The very first lesson that Christians need to learn is love, *love, love.* Love your friends, love those who don't love you, love everyone. And say, do you mind your own affairs, or are you always butting in on other people's business? Jimmy didn't have many friends and didn't know why, until one day his teacher had a talk with him.

"Jimmy," she said, "do you know why the other boys don't seem to like you, and why you don't get your work done in school? It's because you're always interfering with others instead of. doing your own work quietly."

Jimmy really wanted to be liked, so after that he tried sticking to his own job. It worked!

GOOD ADVICE FOR TODAY:

Don't be a goat, always butting in on others. Do your own job quietly and well.

READ I THESSALONIANS 4:13-18.

What If It Were Today!

It's hard to say good-by to a dear friend or loved one, and to attend the funeral service. But what if you had *no hope* of ever seeing that one again? Surely then your sorrow would be unbearable. What a wonderful hope Christians have! Death is only a sleep, from which Jesus will one day waken all who are His own. With beautiful new bodies they will rise to meet Him. If we are His, we shall not be left behind. In a split second these bodies of ours will be changed, and we, too, shall rise to meet our dear Saviour. There will be no good-by's after that, because we shall be with Him, and with those we love forever and ever. Isn't that something to look forward to? And listen! It might happen *today*. Are you ready?

A QUESTION FOR TODAY:

> Glorious hope, He is coming again,
> We shall meet Him in the air;
> Some yet alive, and some who have died—
> Say! shall I meet *you* there?

—M. L. M.

Stay Awake

Jesus is the Light of the world. When we open our hearts to Him, He takes all the darkness of sin away and makes us "children of light." Isn't that a lovely name for Christians? And children of light show to whom they belong by the way they act. We should be wide awake all the time (v. 6), watching lest Satan lure us into one of his traps, watching to see what good we can do, watching for a chance to tell someone about the Lord, watching for the coming of our Lord. Children of light should never pay back any meanness or unkindness (v. 15). We should live so close to Him that we talk to Him about everything, not only on our knees at bedtime, but as we walk, play, or sit in school (v. 17). And no matter what happens, we should say, "Thank You, Lord, I know You have a reason for this" (v. 18). Yes, children of light are really happy!

If we walk in the light, as he is in the light, we have fellowship one with another, and the blood of Jesus Christ his Son cleanseth us from all sin.—I John 1:7

II Thessalonians

In his first letter to the Thessalonians Paul had said a lot about the coming again of the Lord Jesus. You will remember it is mentioned in every chapter. The Christians at Thessalonica were greatly comforted by this wonderful promise of again seeing their loved ones who had died. But they didn't understand that it might not be for quite a while yet. A few of them had insisted that Jesus was coming within a very short time; in fact so soon that they urged others to give up their jobs and just wait for Him. They said this is what Paul had advised them to do. Paul was troubled about all this, and wrote this second letter to put them straight. We'll look over his shoulder to get some idea of what is in the letter.

READ II THESSALONIANS 2:13-17.

Hold On

When we truly love the Lord, Satan has a hard time trying to get us to do things we know are wrong; but he has tricky ways. The people in this church at Thessalonica loved the Lord Jesus very much, and were even suffering persecution for His sake (1:4). They were longing for His return to earth, because that would be the end of their suffering. Then those who were causing them trouble would be punished. Now along comes Satan speaking through some people who claim to be Christians, and they say: "Jesus is coming right away. Paul said so. God tells us so. Don't bother with your job any more. You won't need it." And so some fine, earnest Christians started sitting around doing nothing but talk, while other people had to feed them. Paul had to tell them not to listen to everyone who came along. He said, "Stand firm, hold on to the things I taught you" (v. 15), get busy and work (see 3:10).

TODAY'S TIP:

> Live as if Jesus were coming back today,
> but work as if it would be a long time yet.

READ II THESSALONIANS 3:1-5.

How to Be a Winner

Satan is strong, but God is stronger. We need to remember this when we become discouraged and think that we can never be the kind of Christian God wants us to be. You see even Paul asked people to pray for him, that he might be kept safe from his wicked enemies (vv. 1, 2). We aren't strong enough to stand up against Satan and all his clever temptations, but all we need to do is admit our weakness and trust in our mighty, conquering Lord. Yes, He is *faithful* (v. 3). He will keep us from evil and will give us strength to do what is right. Elijah's servant was scared to death one morning when he saw that he and his master were completely surrounded by enemy soldiers. But Elijah prayed, "Oh, God, open his eyes!" Then he saw. Between them and their enemies were thousands of protecting angels. So it is with us; Satan is strong, but God is stronger.

A BIBLE VERSE FOR TODAY:

If God be for us, who can be against us?
—Romans 8:31 b.

I Timothy

When Paul was in the city of Lystra during his first missionary journey some very exciting things happened. Acts 14:8-11 tells of the healing of the crippled man, and of how the people first wanted to worship Paul, but tried later to stone him to death. Timothy was a young boy in Lystra at that time, and no doubt he had seen what happened to the crippled man, and had listened to Paul preaching. He decided he would believe on the Lord Jesus as his Saviour. When Paul came to Lystra again on his second missionary journey, Timothy was so happy to see him; and when Paul asked him if he would be willing to leave his home and all his friends to be his missionary helper, Timothy was overjoyed. From that very day he became Paul's faithful partner in the work, and the great apostle loved him as if he were his own son.

When Paul realized he would not have much longer to serve the Lord, he asked Timothy to stay in Ephesus and look after the church he had started there. So Timothy was a young minister, and I and II Timothy are letters written to him by Paul to give him some advice that would help him to be a better pastor.

Let's read a little from Paul's first letter to Timothy now.

Not a Pretty Picture

I can imagine Paul blushing with shame as he brings out this old picture of himself to show Timothy. Not very good-looking, is it? A man who used the precious name of Christ as a swear word, who tormented Christians and insulted the Son of God! Yes, Paul says it—and we believe it—he was one of the world's worst sinners. Yet Jesus saved him, cleansed him, and even gave him strength to be a useful and faithful servant. Why? So that everyone can look at Paul and say, "If the Lord Jesus could change him so completely, there's hope for me!" God made an example of Paul, so no one could ever doubt His mercy, and love, and patience with the worst sinner. How it would thrill Timothy to realize what the Gospel had done for Paul! He would be so glad God had called him as a young man to preach such good news.

A CHORUS FOR TODAY:
>Paul would have liked this one:
>"Thank You, Lord, for saving my soul."

READ I TIMOTHY 4:6-10.

Keeping Fit

Do you suppose the world's top athletes sit around eating, smoking and doing as they please? You couldn't possibly be an athlete that way. In order to be strong you must train your body by eating the right kind of food, and by proper exercise. No one can be an athlete without careful training. But do you realize your soul needs training, too, if you are to be a strong Christian? Paul told Timothy: "Train your soul to live for God" (v. 7, Laubach). This is far more important than training our bodies, because we need our bodies only while we are here on earth, but our souls will never die. What are some of the rules to follow so that we shall have healthy souls? First, eat the right food—God's Word—and eat a good square meal every day. One meal on Sunday won't last all week. Then we must exercise—that's putting God's Word into action, being kind, honest, pure, loving. Another good exercise for our souls is witnessing to others about our wonderful Saviour.

Is your soul as healthy as your body? If not, start the right training *today*.

READ I TIMOTHY 6:6-10.

How to Be Rich

Perhaps you are saying, "Think of all I could buy if I had lots of money!" But wait a minute. When you take your last journey from earth to Heaven, what can you take with you? Just what you brought with you when you came into the the world as a tiny baby—nothing! And supposing you had loads of money, the chances are ten to one that you would have loads of trouble, too. Paul says those who love money and crave riches are faced with terrible temptations, and often lose their faith in God. There's something far better than riches, and it's well worth all your efforts to get it. When you have it, you are really rich. What is it? The answer is in verse 6: "godliness" and "contentment," which means a life that is pleasing to God, plus a contented mind—contented with whatever God sends you, and not always wanting something else.

WHEN YOU PRAY:

> Try thanking the Lord for what you have, and, for once, not asking for anything more.

111

Read I Timothy 6:11-14.

Run!

There are times when it is cowardly to turn and run, but sometimes it is the only wise thing to do. Paul warns Timothy to run as fast as he can from things like pride, quarreling, the love of money. If we play around with things like this we're going to get hurt for sure. And there are some things we should chase after and never stop till we catch them. The list is in verse 11: "right living, a Christlike life, faith, love, patience, gentleness." Have you caught some of these? You'll never get them by sitting down and wishing you were like that. You must do something about it. You will often need to be a brave soldier and fight for what you know to be right. Jesus gave a good witness before Pilate; He will help you to be brave, too.

A VERSE FOR TODAY:

When you are tempted to do wrong,
It's often wise to run;
And sometimes you will have to fight,
The battle must be won.

112

So get into the race, my friend,
Your eyes on Jesus—run!
To catch such things as love and peace,
Until the race is done.

—M. L. M.

II Timothy

So far as we can tell this is the last letter written by the great apostle Paul. He wrote it from a prison in the city of Rome. Timothy, who loved Paul very dearly, must have treasured it all his life, because soon after Paul wrote it he went Home to Heaven. I'm glad Timothy kept these two letters carefully. God meant them to be part of our Bible because they will help us to be better Christians; so let us read a few passages from this second letter to Timothy, asking God to bless it to our hearts.

READ II TIMOTHY 1:1-7.

Timid Timothy

Do you know some older Christian who loves you and prays daily for you, as Paul did for Timothy? If so, thank God for such a friend. Supposing some day he tells you of something in your life that needs changing if you are to be a better Christian. Listen and take advice! A real friend tells us the truth even if it hurts. Paul told Timothy he was full of joy when he remembered how deep and real his faith was. But Timothy had one fault. Because he was so young he was sometimes afraid to speak up. Paul reminded him that when he was saved God's Spirit came to live in him, and was like a flame in his heart. "Now fan the flame," Paul wrote; "don't let it die out!" God's Spirit wanted to make Timothy strong, loving and brave.

TODAY'S QUESTION:

Are you a "timid Timothy" or a "daring Daniel"? Remember, if you let God's Spirit have His way in you, you need never be afraid of anyone or anything.

Ashamed

Jimmy's dad died when he was quite small, and his mother worked very hard to get him everything he needed. The public schools at that time were attended only by children from poor homes. Jimmy's mother was determined that her boy should go to the finest boarding school in the country. She worked and saved until she had enough money to cover his expenses, but this left very little to buy clothes and food for herself. One day when Jimmy was away at school she decided to pay him a surprise visit. On arrival she spotted him among a group of boys on the playground, and joyfully made her way toward him. Some of the boys, seeing the poorly dressed little lady, began to make unkind remarks. I still burn with anger at the next part of the story. Jimmy actually pretended not to know his own dear mother! Wasn't that awful? But not worse than being ashamed of our wonderful Saviour. Paul told Timothy never to be ashamed of Jesus. In verse 12 he tells why he is not ashamed of Him.

A Poem for Today:

> Ashamed of Jesus! that dear Friend
> On whom my hopes of Heav'n depend?
> No; when I blush, be this my shame,
> That I no more revere His name.

READ II TIMOTHY 2:1-5.

A. W. O. L.

Every serviceman knows what A.W.O.L. means. Do you? It stands for *Away Without Leave.* In the army it is a very serious offense. It means that a man who has enlisted as a soldier and promised to obey all the rules has broken his word and taken time off without permission. Perhaps he got tired of taking orders from his superior officer. Perhaps he just wanted to have a good time. So he did what he felt like doing, instead of obeying. There are Christian soldiers who are A.W.O.L. They would rather do as they please than serve the Lord and obey Him. Perhaps they are afraid to stand up and take it when their friends laugh at them for going to Sunday school and church. No soldier who is A.W.O.L. will get a reward from the Commanding Officer.

A PRAYER POEM:

> I want to be a soldier, Lord,
> A soldier brave and true.
> I want to please the One I love
> In everything I do.

The enemy is strong, I know.
Alone I cannot stand;
But You have promised grace and strength,
Oh, Saviour! hold my hand.

—M. L. M.

Clean Dishes

Did you ever sit down to a meal at the table and find that your cup was already dirty? Disgusting! That cup found its way to the kitchen sink fast. I don't care if the cup from which I drink is bone china or dime store, so long as it is *clean*. In these verses Paul is reminding Timothy that in a house all kinds of kettles and dishes are used. Some are fine-looking and expensive; others are just ordinary kitchenware. But if they are not clean, they cannot be used. It is not important whether you are rich or poor, a doctor or a cook, but it is very important that your heart be *clean*. Bad habits like lying, cheating, disobedience, make us unfit for the Lord to use us. Boys and girls who allow sins like this to soil their hearts are more like garbage cans than clean cups! Paul tells Timothy to run away from sin (v. 22). That's the only safe thing to do.

WHEN YOU PRAY:

Ask God to take all sin from your heart so that you may be like a clean cup, filled to the brim with His love.

READ II TIMOTHY 3:10-15.

From Bad to Worse

When people turn away from God they find themselves on a road with a steep downgrade. At first they told just little "white lies" (they're really all black!), and deceived only a few people, but they soon found that it takes one lie to cover up another—a bigger lie each time. Yes, they go from bad to worse. When Timothy read these words from his dear friend, Paul, he could just see him looking right into his eyes and urging him to stay on the right road, the road that goes straight on and ends in the Gloryland. It would take backbone, because some of these deceivers would be sure to make trouble for him. Christians must expect that. But if we make God's Word our constant companion, loving it and reading it every day, we shall have strength to keep on living for God.

A CHORUS FOR TODAY:

> I have a wonderful treasure,
> The gift of God without measure,
> And so we'll travel together,
> My Bible and I.

READ II TIMOTHY 4:6-8, 16-18.

In the Jaws of a Lion

Have you ever seen a lion tamer put his head right into a lion's mouth? Scary sight, isn't it? Paul says that is what happened to him, and the lion wasn't a tame one. Yes, you guessed it— Satan. Paul was a prisoner in Rome. Emperor Nero was a cruel man who killed thousands of Christians. Paul knew that very soon it would be his turn to die for Jesus' sake, and he was eagerly looking forward to what he calls his "departure" (v. 6). There was a crown waiting for him, and best of all, he would be with the Saviour he loved so dearly. But until the moment when he would hear Him say, "Welcome Home, Paul," he knew that God would rescue him out of Satan's jaws, as He had done at that first trial. He says not a single person took his side, and Satan thought he had him scared to death. But right beside him stood the Lord Himself, and that gave Paul courage to witness bravely for Him.

Paul would rather have died a thousand deaths than fail to speak a word for Jesus. Do you love Him that much?

Titus

On a map of Europe, find the little Island of Crete, southeast of Greece. That is where Titus was pastor of a church when Paul wrote this letter to him. Titus had a special place in his heart because he had brought him to know the Lord as his Saviour. Like the letters to Timothy, this one was written not long before Paul went to be with the Lord. Paul felt Titus needed a little fatherly advice because he had a difficult church in which to work. Cretans had a bad name. They were known far and wide to be lazy and crooked. Paul knew that Cretan Christians would have a harder fight against bad habits than other Christians, and he wrote to advise Titus how to help them to be strong and true. Here is a page from this short letter.

READ TITUS 3:1-8.

Clean Up

Lazy liars. Excuse the ugly words, but that is just what these Cretan Christians were before they were saved (1:12). They didn't have to clean up their lives before they came to the Lord Jesus for forgiveness. No, we are saved by faith in what the Lord did for us on the cross, not by our good works. We are to come as we are. But when we are saved, it matters very much how we live. Paul tells Titus to remind them of this, and to warn them not to be lazy any more (v. 1), not to tell lies about others, not to quarrel, but to be gentle and very polite to everyone (v. 2). Those who have a job must do their work faithfully, never stealing even the smallest thing, and not answering back (2:9, 10). Our lives must be so clean that those who know us will have to admit that Christ really changes people.

A THOUGHT FOR TODAY:

> Did you ever hear someone say, "Well, if being a Christian makes Bill like that, I don't want to be one"? May it *never* be said of me.

124

Philemon

This is the shortest of Paul's letters. It was written to Philemon, the owner of the slave Onesimus. Onesimus had run away from his master, and while in Rome had found the Lord as his Saviour through listening to Paul. He knew, now that he was a Christian, that he must go back to Philemon and confess all that he had done wrong. Would Philemon punish him severely? He and Paul talked it over, and I can imagine Paul saying, "Well, my son, no matter how hard it will be, you must go back to your master; but I know Philemon, and I'll write a letter for you to take to him. Don't worry; just trust the Lord." Onesimus went. This is the letter he carried in his pocket.

READ PHILEMON 10-12, 15-19.

A Runaway Slave

Can you see Paul seated in his bare little cell in the prison at Rome, white-haired and stoop-shouldered? How loving and courteous his letter is! I think Philemon was probably a hard master before he became a Christian. One day Onesimus couldn't stand it any longer, so he stole some money and ran away. But he found out he couldn't run away from a bad conscience, and when he heard Paul preaching about forgiveness of sin, he accepted the Lord as his Saviour. Right away he was a changed man. Now came the hard part. How could he go back to his master and confess all that he had done wrong? Paul sent this letter to Philemon to tell him that Onesimus was really Onesimus (meaning "useful") now. He begged Philemon to love him and even to release him from being a slave. It is thought that Philemon did release him, and that Onesimus became a useful Christian minister.

Moody Press, a ministry of the Moody Bible Institute, is
designed for education, evangelization and edification.
If we may assist you in knowing more about Christ and
the Christian life, please write us without obligation to:
Moody Press, c/o MLM, Chicago, Illinois 60610.